Your cybersecurity is your own responsibility.

INTRODUCTION

There are many ways to show up at the wrong place, at the wrong moment...

In Netherlands sometime before WWII government wanted to update it's census records, by collecting names of people and their religious views in order to provide better financial support to religious organizations in the country. The idea was to provide religious organizatios with necessary funding appropriate to it's number of supporters. The more people belonged to organization - the bigger amount of money it supposed to receive from government. When on May 10, 1940 Nazi invaded Netherlands, they had all the cencus records they needed, gathered for them for free by Netherlands government. Only 10% of Jewish population of that country survived in World War 2. Without that census records available - the number of survivors could possibly be much higher.

Information that is being collected for the reason of doing good for people could also be used against those same people, if that information ends up in wrong hands. That's the lesson we should learn from history.

Information harvesting methods improved rapidly during last two decades - the era of digital devices and services. This phenomenon has no precedent, this phenomenon simply had not existed before. You are not filling any papers, not completing any surveys, not letting anyone know about your future plans, and yet, somehow the newly installed "free image exchange app" on your phone offering you that nice 5 carat diamond engagement ring, and coincidentally you have planned to make a proposal within next month.

We are making a huge mistake by underestimating a number of information (Data) produced by us every day, every minute. We know that big brother is watching us, but who is that big brother nowadays? Is it NSA? Is it Aliens?

I think that the modern big brother is an Artificial Intelligence, don't get me wrong I am not a futurist or something. By AI I mean computers and systems that are programmed for harvesting, sorting and analyzing data received from different sources. The sources are the sensors that can receive any type of information and transform it to zeros and ones.

Voice, music, movements, geolocation, imaging, you name it. Modern databases can contain all of it.

If it'd be possible to ask your phone company to provide you a full report of your activity in an excel format for last half of a year - you'd be surprised how much they know. That excel file would be as big as 30,000 rows. And if we transform this file to a readable view, we would be able to say what time you woke up. Where you go for work. Your favorite shopping place. Your lunch time and menu. Where you spend time and how long it takes. Names of people you spend time with. When and where you travel.

And all of it is stored in the Internet. All accessible. And all of it is stored and accessible, because you have a smartphone, that sends a signal to the nearest 3-4-5G antenna tower every 1 to 5 minutes. The signal basically represents a status request: is there anything new for me there? Any new emails, new text or update? What's going on in the world right now? And that same signal is also a status report: I am here! I am here now! Look, here I am!

Same thing with all those free email accounts and free storage companies and apps. They give you free access, and after a bit, when you get used to the app, they start asking you for different kinds of permissions. Do you want to give access to your photos? Do you want to give access to your current location? Do you want to give access to your microphone? Camera? Contacts? Yeah, yeah, yeah, they need it to sell better. Why is "Simple Arcade Game" app asking me if I want to let them track my location? To sell that data to a third party. Algorithms that are watching us - do not care about our personalities at all, because they are just programs, not people. Our digital profiles are created automatically, and they exist. However, no one alive is looking at it. But. If someday someone will look at it and the fortune is not on your side - your profile will become your dossier.

Imagine living in the country where drug cartels have access to corrupted phone companies data and can see who is contacting police.

Or, imagine one thousand people standing on a square, demanding a "peace, not war" or someones impeachment or anything else, these are just examples. If we'd have data for every person with smartphone in that crowd - we'd be able to say: who are the leaders in the crowd, how many people are in the crowd and who are those people, their names, addresses and interests, when each person came to the square, from which location and with whom, and with whom they left. With all that we (theoretically of course, if we can take control over phone company) could isolate leaders by turning off the telecommunication for particular people in the crowd, like those that collect more people around them, measured by distance. Or like one Eastern European country government did back in 2014, we can send a warning text message to every participant of the crowd saying: "You've been registered as a participant of illegal manifestation".

We act differently, when we know that we are being watched.

We should not be scared of or blame NSA, governments or enthusiastic startups and ambitious software giants whatever intentions they have. The problem is in the data that is being shared. Just the existence of that data is making us vulnerable and we never know what it can be used for.

From the times of George Orwell's "1984" novel (where people were constantly notified that they are being watched, even when not watched) - it is known that big brother (not sure who is Big Brother nowadays...) is looking for different ways of social control. Difference now is you don't need to be told if you are being watched all the time, you know it, sometimes you're just not aware it is actually happening 100% of your time.

It is time to act, it is time to build some protection and create real privacy in our digital world. And we should not wait until someone come and fix it for us, no one is putting curtains on your windows for you, especially from the outside. And whenever someone asks for our information - the only acceptable way should be for them to get a court warrant.

Cybersecurity is the word understood by the most average computer users as something that the only experts should know about, and regular people shouldn't. It is not a true statement. When "hacking stuff" happens - you are not able to call someone to help. Your data is stolen. What data? Whatever information you kept on electronic devices, and whatever information you had recorded by cameras, GPS, Wi-Fi, bluetooth, microphones and displays on your electronic devices. The technology nowadays play the key role not just in enterprise, business and government sectors - it plays major role in our personal lives. Even if you consider yourself an average user of the household items, such as Apple, Amazon or Android smart systems, flat screen modern TV sets and gaming consoles. There is always either a camera, Wi-Fi or microphone installed in those devices, meaning that it could possibly transfer whatever data is being captured to either the servers of the company that produced the device for further analysis, or to a hacker that had bad intentions. Why bad? Because hacker never asked you if thats ok to use or record/stream your data. Which is probably illegal in many countries. That alone should be enough for you, the rest - lets leave it to our imagination...

The purpose of this handbook is to inform you about possible digital threats to your personal life, when you are using electronic device. Not to make you feel or act "paranoid" about it, but to make sure that you know what you are doing when clicking that link in your email, or downloading that file somewhere in the deep web, or simply giving your kids the wrong type of access on your home internet network, buying your spouse a "mint condition" smartphone from eBay user with 32 positive feedback count. It is not dangerous to do so, if you know what you are doing and what type of responsibility you are taking.

In a recent year 2018 there were many interesting events. Not all of them are getting to the TV on prime time news. Something like biggest data breaches do not stay long in the newsfeed so we may forget or won't even notice it had ever happened. These kinds of events are screwing companies' (data holders') reputation resulting in major changes in its' stock price, financials and customer base. Why not try to resolve this by making news disappear? Why not try to resolve this by giving customers free membership for a year? That's what CEOs think. What I think: Why not just keep security level so high - no-one can steal any data? I know, I know, it's impossible...Then why not pay customers for their future losses caused by the data breach? Especially when you are crazy rich and aware that there is a big possibility that your company's collection of data is kind of a tasty bit for hackers. I think it could be a good idea to create an insurance fund for victims of a data breach. And make every company that participates in personal data harvesting and storage (almost every company) to pay a "per customer" fee to that fund. So when there is data breach - those victims who had their data stolen from company, would receive a compensation for losses, and if that is not enough to cover victims' real loss after all - get more from that fund. And if the fund don't have enough money - raise the "per customer" fee for participating companies. If you agree - let me know.

Now lets see what happened between 2014 and 2018. Some of the companies that had their users' data leaked or stolen.

British airways, the flight company had a data breach with 380,000 users affected. Hack took place on the company's website and it's mobile app. Orbitz, the travel website had a data breach with 880,000 users affected between January 2016 and December 2017. Hackers attacked through company's website. Personal data such as credit card information, addresses, and phone numbers of customers was stolen. SingHealth – the Singapore government's health database attacked by hackers. The target was Singapore's Prime Minister health information. But many more users were affected by the hack. August 2018 T-Mobile – 2 million users affected, an international group of hackers gained access to T-Mobile servers. Hackers got personal data and passwords of the users. March 2018, Cathay Pacific Airways – more than 9 millions passengers data including 860,000 passport numbers, 245,000 Hong Kong identity card numbers. From July 2017 to September 2018 Hackers found vulnerabilities in the Facebook's code and gained full access to 29 million users' data that included sensitive information such as user's location, relationship status, devices used and recent searches.

Wall Street Journal reported, that a software glitch caused Google to expose data of over 500,000 users. The company experienced another security breach that compromised data of approximately 52.5 million users. After the recurrent hacking incidents, Google announced that it would shut down Google+ for good by April 2019. A Facebook app "This is your digital life" provided access to third parties including the Cambridge Analytica, a data analytics firm.

Cambridge Analytica assisted in creating targeted ads during President Trump's presidential campaign. According to data provided by Facebook: 270,000 users use the personality prediction app. However, since Facebook allows sharing of data, this app was able to gather data of millions of other users as well. February 2018 – MyFitnessPal, 150 million users affected - confidential account information including addresses and passwords was stolen. Marriott Starwood hotels- 500 million users. For approximately 327 million of these guests, the information included some combination of name, mailing address, phone number, email address, passport number, Starwood Preferred Guest account information, date of birth, gender, arrival and departure information, reservation date, and communication preferences. For some, the information also included payment card numbers and payment card expiration dates, but the payment card numbers were encrypted using Advanced Encryption Standard encryption. For the remaining guests, the information was limited to name and sometimes other data such as mailing address, email address, or other information. 1.1 billion users affected in Aadhar - the Indian government portal that stores information of its residents. Biometric information leaked so anyone had access to obtain information from the Aadhar website. The information included names of the Indian residents, their ID card numbers, and bank accounts.

For more information on data breaches over the last decade - just go to Wikipedia and search for "list of data breaches". You will be surprised how much data was stolen.

What do you think are the chances your data got stolen, and no-one told you about it?

So is it good or bad that companies are aggressively harvesting data, while we are busy figuring out our work/life balance?

I would say it's both, but to me dark side outweighs the good side. Because good side that I see from user perspective is - they use data mostly to make shopping experience easier by advertising goods that I was looking for and didn't know the legit place I could find it at. The fingerprint sensor on my phone? Well I don't see this as anything really important, since most popular smartphone companies decided to exclude it from their newer smartphones, after collecting all fingerprints with older smartphone versions of course. What a nice excuse of not having it because the screen is actually taking whole front side of the phone. The million-dollar-a-year-paid engineers couldn't figure out how to put that elsewhere. Yeah, right. And now when they have all fingerprints - they want to see how your face looks, in 3D. So precise, that only twins or kids could fake it.

The dark side to me looks a lot bigger and I should say "brighter", but it's only "brighter" for maybe investors of those companies, since data brings money and it is so easy to harvest it. It is not brighter for us, simple users. What does "like" means nowadays in digital world? It is an opinion shared. When you like someones post or video you basically saying you are supporting such activity in a content posted, unless you are liking your Mom's instagram post of new flowers she put in a backyard garden, that could be seen as you just supporting the family, not necessary the activity itself. But we can understand a lot, when we see who "liked" what, right? Imagine what modern AI can do. It can collect all your opinions in one database. So the data purchaser, if it knows that you like cats, especially siamese breed ones, could make a targeted ad and show it to you on one of the social networks. Imagine that you are going though your updated newsfeed on social network and see your least favorite politician petting a siamese cat, or doing whatever you adore. Would you change your mind regarding that politician for at least a bit? I will. What if the same campaign shows you that politician going for a hike? And you are a hiker. That would be the next step of changing your mind. The number of steps needed to be done to fully change your mind on a specific topic depends on current voting opinion polls. And all that it costs is just to purchase the database of all collected "likes" and "reposts" of specific country's citizens and look for most popular ones. Most popular doesn't mean most important. It is needed for creating sympathy, make you more attracted to something. Do you now really want to share any of your opinions like that? We can already see results in news, how data could be manipulated. The data you produced. We hate free pop-up surveys and try to avoid it in most cases, but we are easily and honestly filling out a non-paid global infinite survey of our deepest secrets, habits and desires.

PART 1. DEVICES.

From the end of 20th century the most popular digital device for modern human is phone. We should all say a big thank you to Steve Jobs for creating smartphone that is really "smart" in 21st century, it gave so much to so many people, some got new job as an app developer, some started playing games and watching movies in the train on their way to and back from work, chatting with friends around globe, many businesses built their business model based solely on smartphone use. Smartphone is not evil. Smartphone is a tool. Now, imagine you have a great Swiss army knife that does lots of things, it opens cans and bottles and does your nails. I would say smartphone is a "Swiss army knife" for whatever social stuff you have. By social I mean interacting with others and also entertaining yourself by interacting with "Ai".

Siri or Alexa make you socialize with "AI" for example. Can I say that? So smartphone is a great tool for that. Not that long ago we used regular phones purely for communication reasons and had paid for minutes of talking time. Our conversations could be recorded, text messages could be read and also our locations could be tracked by using 2g or 3g antennas. Thats how special forces were tracking some of the worst criminals of the world, they used all three recording methods to find a person. Lets put it this way, let's assume that Special forces are the company with one purpose - mine as much data as it can from the target device. Let's assume that those bad guys are the company with one purpose - make sure that no data could be mined from their devices. These two companies are always in competition mode. The bad guys' company knows that data it produces costs a lot of money for governments to harvest. Price of theis data is high. And no one willing pay bad guys for that data. Governments are willing to pay for that data to 3rd party companies that could harvest it. Because if government purchase data straight from its producer - the data loses it's value. Data will not have any true values in it. Only history. To imagine that - Special forces are calling the drug lord and asking to send a database of all locations where transactions are made and also send all planned locations pins on map for the next 2 years. Drug lord will send the database to Special forces and charge hundred thousand dollars for it. What is the value of that data to Special forces? Now they know where drug transactions took place. Now they also know where drug transactions will not take place for sure. What can they do about it? Nothing towards the quick and smart decision and action to catch Drug lord. They can, at most analyze the history data and try and produce some forecast patterns with many unknown variables. When Special forces want to buy data from a hacker - this same data will bring a lot of value. It will basically do all the job for them. They would need to just act fast and come and arrest Drug lord at the specified location at specified time gathered from stolen Drug lord's database. No analysis needed.

So it is a Drug lord's responsibility to:

a) Produce less data: the less data - the more analysis needs to be done - the more money needs to be invested - the more time needed to find that money - the more time available to do bad stuff.

b) Protect the data: the more data protected - the more time needed to mine it. It is never impossible, it just takes more time.

So how is it, produce less data? Does Drug lord need to speak less? Move less? That's not going to help business. So it is not an option.

Produce less data means produce just enough amount of data that is required to stay alive and do business.

After part A done, comes part B, they don't go independently, these two parts should be done together, one after another.

Part B could be anything from encrypting data to making sure data is completely erased after usage. Like when you clear your browsing history.

Encrypting is a smart word, that many companies use, but from my perspective - encryption is just a nick name for your password and a nickname does not work if you don't use your own memory as a side key to decrypt that nickname. So the Drug lord can use nickname for the locations used for transactions, like "Garage" could be a nickname for a place that used to be a big downtown car garage in 1980s and only few people remember it, all of which are Drug lord's employees. So to decrypt nickname they need their own memory. If you don't have that data, it is impossible to say with more than 1 percent confidence that it's that exact place. Too many unknown variables.

Why am I talking about criminals and special forces? This book is not a handbook for criminals, neither it is a handbook for special forces. It is a hand book for average digital device users. It's just, criminals and special forces make the best example of real competition for data producers and data miners. Because there is basically no competition between miners and producers in nowadays social life. It is more like monopoly then competition. All data mining done with all the corporate money and average user is just a producer that is being milked in any way possible and don't have enough resources to substitute main services offered by data mining companies. If user does not want to let miners mine - then s/he can't get any services, if s/he can't get services - then her/his life quality will be less then average data producer's that decided to share his/her data for services in exchange. Unless you are crazy rich.

You want to take a ride to airport. What do you do?

a. Use Ride sharing app

b. Take train

c. Ask your friend or family member to give you a ride.

d. Take a cab

C is a rare event. At least for me. Train? Maybe. But only if the train station is located next to my house. If not, I get uber at least to get to the train. No cabs, I will need to call to request, then price is not clear beforehand, and I'm cheap. Now, what data will I share? Please take a minute and write down all data that you can possibly produce by using Ride sharing app and train to get to airport. I assume you answered this question at least in your mind, otherwise - this is first sign of not willing to become aware, gotcha.

In my humble opinion the data I would produce contains, but not limited to:

- My Credit card information

- My First and Last name

- My exact location right now, before I agreed to ride.

- Probably my whole trip to airport, so Ride sharing app knows I made that train trip to go to airport. Because in rare case I remember to close the app from background or at least turn off location services right after my car ride is over.

- Thats it?

Only if your smartphone has 1 app installed on it.Who will also know your location? Your phone manufacturer and your phone company. They have all the power to have it. They use your device as much as you do, if not more. Now what if you have any app that you are using for texting and talking, browsing Internet and sharing pictures? You may think Whatsapp or maybe Instagram or Facebook, they all belong to Facebook anyways...And of course you have camera access granted and your microphone access granted for whatsapp. Don't you use those apps? Ok how about iMessage? How about Photos app? Or how about having microphone and 3 cameras with face identification and a fingerprint sensor on a side. These are not apps. These are tools that apps use on your smartphone. If you start guessing how much data you shared during your trip from home to airport - you could as well imagine where is the end of the universe and how does it look. And we know it's hard to think about it and hard to imagine. So we basically try not to think about it too much - in order to not make our mind break. I am not being paranoid, I am just imagining that this is a good strategy for data harvesters to make data producers (us, users) think less on that matter - think less of amount data we produce and send it away for free, partially against own will. It's just too much stuff to keep in mind to think about it..right? Some might even not think they are producing any data at the moment...they are too busy playing 3rd level of their favorite "diamonds" game. And remember - all that data is not even your history. This data is your "now", it is your real-time data! The Drug lord is upset. You just gave it away. Again - with having real-time data, digital systems and AI could act faster to respond - they are "Special forces". How they respond - is strictly the decision of the company that posses the data. If it's a sales app - they use it for better sales, if it's a ride share app - they use it for better sales, if it's a game app - they use it for....right, better sales. By sales I mean they either improve their sales methods and try to get more money out of pockets of users, or, they sell data to 3rd parties and 3rd parties use that data to get more money out of pockets of same users by selling their "useless 3rd party stuff". In any case - users will spend more money somewhere. "Data=money". "Time=money". Do not make "time=data" is the ultimate idea of this book. You can stop reading here if you are bored already. Then you miss what else data equals to.

My home is my castle.

The castle doctrine in some countries guarantees a number of rights to an owner of the castle. That includes the right to protect own property. Should I consider information being kept inside my house as my property? And also, should I consider as my property - the information being produced in my house such as any dialogues with my wife and kids, different sounds that I produce, my new song I sing in the morning in the shower, my phone pizza orders, photos and artwork I keep on the walls.

I don't know if I want to protect most of that from virtual intruders that want to see or hear it, but I certainly don't want those virtual intruders whether it is a AI or people, to access my property without proper request for my approval and then proper notice at every moment of time they're doing it, with something like "RECORDING IN PROGRESS" notification.

It is just human psychology that is being adopted partially from "spy" movies and "spy" "breaking news". It is not comfortable to be aware something is going on around you, and you don't understand what is happening and how exactly it is happening.

What is the difference between your friend and the new device you just bought. Your friend that tries to come to your house and read all your physical mail and the device you just bought that records every word you are reading to your wife.

In first case you will notice it and probably make sure your friend will not do this again at least without your permission, in second case you don't even notice it. Second case will be your hidden "friend" from now on. You can easily identify your new "friend", it has either one of these attributes: camera, microphone, 3d space sensor (similar to those Wii activity game consoles). And "friend" has two more almost necessary attributes: wifi or bluetooth or cord connection to internet or your computer, and it consumes electricity. How many "friends" do you have? How many you want to buy soon? I know, I know, it is so cool to put Alexa in your bedroom and make it control all of your lights and tell you the current weather in Antarctica. I am sure one of the consumers myself, and I like where we are going with that. I like cats and I keep one in my house, but I keep in mind it can bite me sometimes while playing, so I'm usually not even angry or feeling too much pain after it does. I just try to master my play with cat, I put a kitchen glove and do all I want, or If I'm in the mood, I'm just trying to be as fast with my hand against cat as I can, but still get bites and scratches. So best strategy would be using a kitchen glove, but it gets boring after a few fights, because I always win. Thank god my devices are not like my cat, and "winning" them all the time wouldn't be boring, because I don't have any positive personal feelings when interacting with them. This is an important part of our lives - to make our house a castle, to feel private. We spend 15 to 30 years to make dream come true by getting a mortgage. We buy stuff and put cameras around to protect it, install security sensors on windows and keep on living in an illusion of privacy. The privacy is nothing more than a known amount of your personal information being distributed at every moment of time. It's like: "How many people know what you are doing right now?"

If you know that 1000 people know and you are ok, then this is privacy. When you don't know that it is actually 1000000 and not 1000 - this is not privacy. In my personal opinion of course. Maybe I'm wrong.

My car is my castle too, by the way.

I remember how I discussed many interesting and important and, sometimes, even business-related topics with my friends and colleagues in road trips.

Car is a sacred space for any car owner. I sometimes even allow myself to smoke a good cigar inside my car, it's so cool. It's like home, it makes your mind relax from work day, be more concentrated on the road, not to control what you say sometimes in the road rage, even if the opponent does not hear. When you are relaxed you are the perfect game for data harvesters. Yeah, I know, right? It's everywhere! Car is still one of the least digital devices you may have, unless it's a brand new one. The reason is lack of constant internet connection, but how much time left to solve this question and connect every car to a modern world? I bet Mr. Musk knows.

I am only describing my point of view here and I will share my ideas further in this book, ideas on how to protect your data, or at least minimize your produced data amount for unwanted recording. But first we should review every aspect of the data movement processes that we are currently in. To be aware first.

AI SUGGESTIONS...

PART 2. YOUR ENVIRONMENT.

While working, traveling, having fun with friends or just chilling at home we may share some of the "personaliest" information with unknown people or services. It is not the same thing as I was writing about before. Before I was writing about data that you share through your devices around, you share it with services that you have installed yourself. In this part I am explaining how you are sharing your data with anonymous receivers. Like hackers and services that are under no obligation on how to use your data. It often may be used as identity theft, private investigation purposes, sales, blackmailing, fraud and whatever it is useful for. So, how does it happen?

Use case 1: *You are sending a picture from your smartphone, made a minute ago, to someone.*

Typical file format for picture is JPEG. JPEG picture file has metadata. Metadata is your file's data. You picture is a file that contains not only the image code, but also the information describing the file itself. Like a driver's license has information of a particular driver. Driver's license is metadata for driver (if we consider driver is just the JPEG picture). Ok back to image.

So metadata of the JPEG file contains such information as GPS location of camera that has taken the picture. JPEG/Exif is the most common image format used by digital cameras and other photographic image capture devices. In JPEG/Exif format, picture Exif APP1 segment stores a great amount of information on photographic parameters for digital cameras and it is the preferred way to store thumbnail images. It can also host an additional section with GPS data. Considering you have a smartphone with GPS, those that have access to your fresh photos - may figure out your current location.

Use case 2: *You are chilling at home, surfing the internet, clicking random links, accessing any random websites.*

IP address is your computer's or router's Internet Protocol address. It contains 4 numbers separated by commas, like 00.00.00.00. It is the language computers and other devices use to communicate online. IP address is unique to your device. It is a part of an internet protocol that allows us to go online. So your IP address is revealed to the World Wide Web. By looking up IP address of the device online you can tell the City it is located in. But if we imagine that we are the internet provider that services the device, then we know the person behind that IP address - the owner of the device.

Use case 3: *You are staying in a vacation rental in a random country.*

Do I really need to tell you that nowadays the size of the

camera could be as small as 8mm by 8mm? If not then I probably won't tell you that it could be used illegally to capture your actions. If you didn't know - please do your own research.

Use case 4: *You are traveling and went through a registration process before your flight.*

If you have Instagram account, you can look for hashtag *#boardingpass* and find many pictures of boarding passes shared by Instagram users. Please never do that. And not even that. Please never dispose your boarding passes, please make sure they are destroyed and are not captured by any cameras or scanners except the ones that your flight operator uses. Why? Because it contains your personal information. Not just first and last name. The barcode could be easily decoded to reveal some of the important information that could be used to change or cancel your flight, use your milage points, and potentially lead to identity theft.

Use Case 5: *You are converting files from one format to another.*

There are many online services (websites) that allow users to quickly convert their pictures (JPEG) to PDF files. Convert PDF to pictures and many more different formats. It is easy and quick. No user agreements to sign. Just leave your email address and upload a document you want to convert. Then you take your recent tax return or W2 scan, and convert it to PDF. Reason? Maybe your accountant asked for PDF, who knows why you need it. No one wants to spend money for add-ons to your PDF reader app, if it's a one time thing, or once a year thing. So you just do it online. The thing is - you don't know where your uploaded data gets stored and who can read it. There are risks for sure. Identity theft risk may be the one to be afraid of.

Use case 6: *You are clicking the link in your email.*

Most known way for hackers to get access to your personal email is to send you the email message that is looking serious and asking that you proceed further by clicking the hyperlink attached. That email message may look like your online banking notification or something as important. It's called 'phishing" - you click the link thinking you need to confirm your banking information and you get transferred to a website that looks exactly like your banking website. You may notice the difference in the webpage's URL (URL is the **http://wwwsomething**....) for the real URLs companies use secured connections, called HTTPS, and not HTTP, as most "phishers" do. So once you enter all the information to confirm your banking details - hackers can use it right away to enter your real banking website and do dirty stuff.

Another way is when you click on one of these links and get transferred to a malicious website that will make your computer infected by a virus, there are dozens different types of viruses you can have, none of them are good. Antiviruses are not always able to detect them.

PART 3. YOUR DIGITAL ASSETS.

Your digital assets are all your online accounts. These include but not limited to: social networks, banking, credit bureaus, cloud storage, online TV, email, shopping sites.

Basically it's anywhere you leave any type of your personal information ("any" means "any", including only your first and last name or your email address) - I personally consider as digital asset.

An **asset** is anything of value or a resource of value that can be converted into cash. **A computerized database isconsidered as Intangible asset. What could computerized database contain? My first name and my last name. That is your personal computerized database with one record, recorded in zeros and ones within a computer.**

Can your Name be an assett? I beliee so, because it's the data, that could be converted into cash. So we can't probably legally call it an asset because it's not a stock or bond or cash, but we can assume it's a digital asset, because that data could be sold on a "data market". You are probably wondering "if my name can be converted into cash - how can I go sell it right now?" There is no way. I mean there's probably a way, but it's not worth it. You only have one name and once you sell it you'll have very little payment. Companies earn by selling thousands or even millions of names collected, thats why it's worth it for them. If someone can't agree that Name or email are asset, then maybe they would agree these are parts that make an asset.

What if there's a Company A with a database of one thousand email addresses and one thousand names connected to it. And it collected the data by asking it's website visitors to sign up using email address. And there is a company B that is collecting opinions online, they ask you to fill the form to leave your opinion whether you like comedy shows or drama.

Company B collected your IP address and your opinion. Company A collected your email address and name.

Company C is the company that sells goods online and has your physical address, it's collected your physical address and name and IP address.

Companies A, B and C mentioned in their user agreements that they would share your information with affiliates. Imagine Company D is their affiliate.

So if Company D can buy data from company A, B and C paying for example penny per account - it will spend 30 dollars for 1000 accounts.

By having IP address it could compare and aggregate and sort data received so it has if not 100% then maybe 50% of data gets sorted correctly, where Company D is certain that 500 accounts it has contain: First and Last name, IP address, physical address, email address, and user preference: drama or comedy. Now that is a very useful information that Company D can sell to another company - Company F. Company F sells magazines. 500 users will soon receive a Drama/Comedy magazine offer in their mail and email. The magazine subscription cost is $20 per year. Even if 30% of that 500 users buy magazine it will bring $300 a year.

The numbers of course are just from my own imagination. It's of course different and lot more complex in real world. My point is to show the simple example of data monetization. So you get my idea why we can consider our names and any other digital information that could be personalized as digital asset.

I think we can classify the types of the digital assets.

I think that there are "insured" and "uninsured" digital assets. In no way I mean insured as they are really under some kind of insurance. I use these terms for myself, I associate them to moments where I am sure that data is protected and not shared with anyone and if lost - I will not be financially harmed.

Now, my classification is a bit complex. Because I don't see any of my digital assets as "insured".

If I lose my banking information - it could be used for stealing money from my account, even knowing that bank will return my money after thorough investigation, it would take time. And we know time equals money.

If I lose my social network account details - it could be used for many purposes including identity theft. And after identity theft - I will spend a great amount of time to put everything together so it looks like before. No need to explain further.

So nothing really is "insured", so why bother making up a classification that does not make sense. Well, to me it makes a great sense, because without classification I will not be able to see that my digital assets or my data really isn't "insured".

Companies promise you that your data input is "encrypted", "protected", "safe", "anonymous" and many more fancy worlds, but they probably won't be able to say it is "insured". Keep that in mind.

Now what if I tell you: your gold that you keep in my house is protected by security guards but not insured, would you trust me your gold? What if I tell you: your gold is hidden somewhere no-one knows, but not insured, would you trust me your gold?

What if I tell you: I promise safety but hold no financial responsibility if I don't provide safety would you think I am a person who's not trying to manipulate your trust?

PART 4. MARKETS.

You might think that "if my personal data (such as name, address and my likes, dislikes or preferences) is harvested, why bother avoiding data production now, since "they" already have it.

The answer is: some of the data may not change over time, like name and ssn. But everything else is updating in your profile every day.

There should be definitely a competition between data harvesting companies. If someone has your data that has been last updated 2 years ago, then probably that someone would only be able to sell the name and ssn part. But not the likes and dislikes, and maybe not even address.

The value of the data is in it's freshness.

Eample of competition between 2 data harvesting companies: Company A has your data updated last month, Company B has your data updated last hour. Which data gets sold faster?
Another example: there are 10000 people that produce data every day.

You are one of them. You are going to stop producing much data during next year until Jan 2020. After Jan 2020 there will be 2 companies selling harvested data, Company A has database dated last year until Jan 2019, and Company B offers same database but updated at the date of sale (end of Jan 2020).

Company A's database is probably won't be sold. Because there's is an updated one that has recent data. You will not be there.

So after a few years lets see what your profile can look like:

First Name - updated 2 years ago

Last Name - updated 2 years ago

Address - updated 2 years ago

SSN - updated 2 years ago

Likes - updated 2 years ago

Dislikes - updated 2 years ago

Favorite daily locations - updated 2 years ago

Shopping - updated 2 years ago

Travel - updated 2 years ago

Friends - updated 2 years ago

Sexual preferences - updated 2 years ago

Police contacts - updated 2 years ago

Work location - updated 2 years ago

Martial Status - updated 2 years ago

Children - updated 2 years ago

Health - updated 2 years ago

What could've change in 2 years?

All of it, and all of it could've change drastically. Who might be interested in such a profile in our modern, constantly changing world? Maybe only KGB or someone alike. But it is much harder to get one specific profile of one person then just a bunch of 10000 random profiles of people who are married, like bikes, have 2 kids, have asthma and work in construction business.

My point is: the less data you produce over time -> the less the chances your profile goes to an updated database for sale -> the less the chances you get manipulated or harmed.
Of course what's been shared is shared forever, and there is nothing you can actually do about it, only learn a lesson.

But there are still a lot of things you can share, and it is better to realize it right now.

Realize that when you created your social network profile back in 2010 and shared all you wanted, you haven't thought that in "One of the greatest countries" border security might start officially checking it in 2020. And it will be considered by government as an optional measure for Border Security Officer to keep homeland secure by basically getting inside your private life details. It hasn't happened by the time i'm writing this book, but there are talks about it everywhere on the Internet news websites.

FYI. Three of the top social networking companies alone make somewhere about $44 billion a year selling consumer data to advertising companies.

Data markets could be legal and illegal. I will not touch legal part. We are at least aware of those.

Illegal data markets are the ones that we often are not aware of.

There are 3 layers of web (internet) you can access. They called: Surface web, Deep web and Dark web.

Surface web is also called Lightnet or Visible Web is the part of the World Wide Web that we can see right away, by using standard internet browser. It is indexed by search engines and can be found in search results. In simple worlds Surface web is any landing web page that does not require login or any additional action to see the information it contains.

Deep web is whatever web page you can't simply land on while using browser or find it in search results is hidden from Surface web. These pages are not indexed by search engines and therefore could only be seen when user passes some type of authentication. For example -your email. You will not see your latest email from your employer asking you to show up tomorrow for 10am meeting, while using just Google search. Thats because those results lay in a deep web layer. And in order to get there you would need to pass the authentication wall (login/password). Same goes for your Netflix or any other account. Authentication wall helps to recognize you and show your personalized data, or to see something else that the company wants to show you but doesn't want to show to everyone who uses search engines. That being said - "Deep web" is the name for the information, available in regular internet, but "kind of" protected by login and password. You are probably accessing deep web one or more times a day, without thinking "deep web", by opening your email account, banking and anything else that asked for your password. I just want you to know that it's called Deep web. Deep web is currently the biggest data storage of all three (surface web, deep web and dark web). Databases, movies, music, books, shopping carts - deep web has currently more than 90% share of what internet has to offer.

Deep web and Dark web are two terms that people usually get confused with.

Dark web is a total different story. The main difference of Dark web is it's anonymity. You can't access it by using your regular browser. You will need to use a special browser that will mask your computer's IP address in order to access Dark web. The webpages there are not indexed, even those that are not protected with authentication wall. You will need to manually enter webpage's address in the address field. Like imagine if you wanted to open your online blog you would have to manually enter http://blablabla...

In Dark web, if you want to access a webpage - you would need to know it's full address and be able to print it in URL field manually.

Dark web is considered the most hidden and anonymous way to surf the internet. That is why it is so attractive to many criminal minded people. And from this book we know why. Criminal minded people are not willing to produce and share much data of their actions.

But because it's attractive to those people shouldn't be the reason of not to use it by regular users. It is just a tool for being anonymous. To be honest if I'd have a oatmeal or granola bar business and needed very secured conversations with my colleagues about my company strategy or some kind of 'secret granola bar" recipe that could cost me millions of dollars if stolen - I would probably consider using Dark net for these conversations.

So my point is - tools are tools, and nothing else. Hammer could be used by a criminal to break the glass of the car to steal a radio, would that stop you from buying hammer to get the framing job done in your basement?

That "Dark Web" tool is used to sell the identity theft and stolen data. It is being sold by hackers to hackers. When you wonder where that stolen Social Network or Cloud storage data goes to - the answer is Dark Web. Obviously, data thieves or hackers rarely use that data for anything else than profits. Otherwise, they would steal less because data they steal is not interesting for them and sometimes it's just not protected enough, so that it makes this data an easy game for a hacker to harvest. If it's a credit card data - then it's being sold to people who can manually use it for stealing money from credit cards, if it's a SSN - they use it for identity theft and so on. The selling part is also protecting harvesters from being identified. When special forces find criminals (who commited identity theft) and put them in jail, the data harvesters are still unidentified and keep hacking data servers. I think it might be a huge pain in the butt for special forces - when the root of the problem is not caught. So it makes those who hack servers more dangerous people than those who buy it. If we can find a hacker who steals it - we can prevent data loss, therefore we can prevent abuse of this data.

When I'm notified my data is stolen from some company's encrypted server it makes me feel just angry and sad. Because I have zero thoughts on where can I go for help to protect myself from any threats that it could lead to. It's too late.

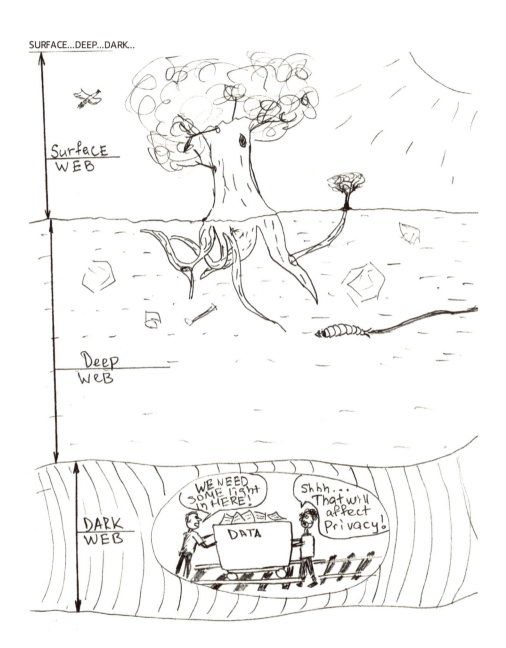

PART 5. TRANSACTIONS.

Your payment history is another type of data. If you look at your main banking account statement for last three or four months, or if you show it to someone - you and they will be able to make a simple analysis by just reading it and come to conclusion about your lifestyle. If you ever got a mortgage approval from your bank - then you know underwriters look at it thoroughly to see what kind of transactions you made just to make sure you are not a risky borrower. It is not easy nowadays to constantly go to bank and get cash every time you do grocery shopping, gas and other basic things, which very well could describe your personality or even the city you reside in, while appearing on your bank statement. Online payments are not even possible to substitute. You always use your credit card - how else can you pay online?

Cryptocurrencies started being "popular" not that long ago. Bitcoin is probably the most famous and controversial asset that we know. Some say it has no future, some say it has big future. Others say it is risky to invest in Bitcoin. And some people still have no idea of what Bitcoin is.

The main thing behind Bitcoin or any other cryptocurrency is a system that allows it to be unique way of payment. It is anonymous and at the same time every transaction is completely transparent and traceable by anyone in the world. This system called Blockchain. Blockchain is a digital ledger system. It has records of every transaction made within it. Each Bitcoin is unique, like every dollar bill. Because it has its own serial number on it. So Blockchain can show that 'bitcoin 1234' "went from wallet A to wallet B on May 1, 2019 at 3pm". It can't show who is the owner of wallet A or wallet B, it can't also show what type of transaction it was (grocery purchase or money transfer or else). Very useful thing if you need to send money to someone. Not a very useful thing if you want to hold it. I am not trying to say Bitcoin or any other cryptocurrency is an investment tool. I am just trying to say that crypto is good to make a payment if you want to pay for something right now and make it anonymously.

It does not matter what cryptocurrency I use, Bitcoin or Litecoin or Ethereum to make a simple payment. The difference is there, but to me it does not matter as long as I am aware my cryptowallet is private and only I know it belongs to me. The difference could be in the type of encryption and many other tech factors, also in of transaction processing times and fees that ledger systems charge for it.

There are 2 ways of buying cryptocurrency.

One way is you go online and open a cryptocurrency account on one of the regulated legal cryptocurrency exchanges. Another way is you get a crypto wallet made for specific cryptocoin and keep it on your computer or on your flash storage card. Yes, flash card can act as cryptowallet. Once you have cryptowallet - you can find someone with bitcoin and just buy it for cash for example, there are many meetups you can find online for people who want to do these kinds of transactions, but you would have to make sure it is legal in your country.

It is, of course, easier to open account on cryptocurrency exchange, online. I consider those accounts are handy only when I am investing, and do not have any intention in doing any transactions where I want to stay private. Because during your registration process you will share your personal information with Cryptoexchange company, and the wallet number that you have will stay connected to personal data and kept somewhere "encrypted" until some smart hacker steals that data.

When you get your wallet downloaded on your computer - you will not share any personal data at least, except your computer's IP address, so I think VPN connection is the best way to download and/or register your wallet online, this way your IP address is masked. We will talk about "what is VPN connection?" later.

You've probably heard that bitcoin value changes rapidly from low to high over short periods of time. During the day it can cost from 3000 dollars to 3400 dollars, the volatility is high. And that it is considered very risky. I agree. But why is it bad to use as payment tool? I don't know.

If I want to buy an ebook sold online - I know it costs 100 bucks. And what if I want to stay anonymous? Then I want to pay with Bitcoin. I don't care how much it costs right now.

It will still equal 100 bucks for me.

To explain what I mean in steps:

1. I see ebook I want to buy online costs $100

2. I want to pay with Bitcoin

3. I have cash

4. I buy zero point something bitcoins from my friend for cash according to current exchange rate

5. My friend sends me zero point something bitcoins to the wallet number I provide

6. As soon as I receive my zero point something bitcoin - I send it as payment for my ebook I want to buy.

7. Seller receives zero point something bitcoin and if seller decides - s/he can convert it back to dollars right away (by selling it for cash or using cryptocurrency exchange, and it will still be worth about 100 dollars).

It is not guaranteed, and volatility risks are still there, but so far I haven't had any problems with volatility paying online with Bitcoin.

That was an example of me using bitcoin not as an investment, but as a payment option only! Keep that in mind. This book is about tools, not investments!

If you are looking for advice - please find professional accredited legal investment advisor elsewhere.

PART 6. HACKERS.

A hacker is a person that can access protected private digital property. Not necessary a bad person as there are Hackers that work for IT security to help organizations find loopholes in their security. Criminal minded hackers sometimes are non-linear thinkers. What I mean by that is they are not always doing dirty stuff only behind their computers, sometimes they act in the field. They could physically install credit card reader inside your favorite grocery store's card machines at every register and stay uncaught, collect enough data and successfully remove those readers, so no one knows they were ever installed. Hackers can also hack one system that is not related to security to break another system that is related to security. For example there was one case in one of my favorite shows, when hacker hacked the A/C system that made the server building overheat that lead to servers with data burn physically. Or something like that... I don't remember exactly, but that does sound legit. And sometimes hackers use your laptop camera to watch you. So please, cover it already.

PART 7. STRATEGIES, STRA-TAGEMS AND TACTICS.

Business or Marketing part of every modern company includes these fancy words.

Sales is the most important thing for every business.

What is the difference between these three words for you right now? Yeah right, too much to discuss. Well for companies these are set. If you ask a company about these 3 words, and that company is very honest about everything it does (which is hardly possible) - then you will receive a clear answer about what would be their strategy, what stratagems they use and what would be tactics for them.

In this part I'm only looking from Business-to-Customer "data sharing" perspective.

Strategy is something that companies use for long term. Like some list of actions that will be taken to achieve its mission.

Strategy example:

A strategy to become a Number one device brand.

- Produce quality product

- Invest big money in marketing

- Keep prices high

The strategy success would make people buy more expensive quality digital devices that may be much overpriced.

Stratagems are more like a specific existing rule (more of a wise sentence, the tactic proven in history for many times) that you can apply to current situation, that fits into this rule and then follow to achieve your short term goals.

Stratagem example:

"Hunt in troubled forest" - I know I am changing the idiom, but this is stratagem, not idiom.

The stratagem used for situations where you can take advantage of chaos in which both you and your enemy are currently stay. Create more chaos around and distract enemy and move silently around to attack from unusual angle.

Businesses apply this stratagem when they see it as the best way to deal against competitors in an unusual market conditions.

Then tactics are something that look like a specific plan of actions to achieve a short term goals.

Example of tactics:

Sell more cheap phones, for less than its' production price , just so one million devices is sold by June 1, 2020, because the price of each device internet traffic usage will cover costs and bring profit.

Thats the tactic for getting bigger costumer base for future use. You may call it "$1 device with a 2-year contract".

Why am I touching this topic is because as customers and, more specifically, data producers - we fall under business strategies, stratagems and tactics playing a subject role.

We fall under strategies when signing up for "popular free photo sharing service". We improve the number of app's active users.

We fall under stratagem when we don't bother trying to turn off location services or microphone access because businesses made settings look hard to set, or hard to access. Result is us sharing more data then actually needed to use app.

We fall under tactics when we turn off access but suddenly appearing banners remind us to turn it on and being tired of looking at it we turn it on.

There are plenty of them, so I won't describe each, these are just to make you aware that it's not an accidental developer mistake that you act, like you act in response to what you see. It is actually in most cases part of a thoroughly planned process, planned by businesses or hackers.

PART 8. NOW THAT YOU ARE AWARE OF SOME ASPECTS OF DATA HARVESTING AND OVERALL MOVEMENT, WHAT CAN YOU DO TO MINIMIZE DATA LEAK?

Now that you are aware of methods that companies and hackers use to harvest your data or exchange your data, it is time to just sit and realize how hard to describe the best way of protection. No wonder companies with thousands of people working in Cybersecurity sector are still somewhat vulnerable and keep on constantly training their employees to act safer.

We know that future is not, or hardly predictable. But some aspects are. Especially when we know history and present time well. What do we know from the past and present? We know that as soon as new technology is invented - it is mostly used for profit or national security. If the new technology costs a lot of money - then it is obvious that someone invested in it's creation, and investors are always looking for profit.

We know that many new inventions, whether it is software or hardware, are made for data harvesting. Invention's mission might be not a "data harvesting" one, but eventually it will harvest it just because it appears feasible to do so.

We know that data could be stolen from well known and "secured looking" companies.

We know that once data is stolen, there is nothing we personally can do to bring it back. Maybe if you are some kind of superhero, then I'm not sure about this one.

We can now try and predict, based on what we know from history and present time.

We can predict that the new app we install could harvest our data.

We can predict that data will probably be sold to 3rd party.

We can predict we will become victims if data stolen.

We can predict that new invention (if it has any type of sensor like microphone or camera or GPS) will share information online.

We can predict that the ways to turn off any data sharing will become harder and harder on these inventions. It will require more and more knowledge to do this for a non-tech savvy users.

If you can predict that you become a victim of identity theft tomorrow - will you be trying to avoid it today, or just forget and let it be?

PART 9. CATEGORIES OF USERS.

I like to categorize stuff. Sometimes more than needed. But here I just want to show how I see categories of the citizens of digital world. I want to categorize them so you can apply, if you want of course, any of the categories to your present time and planned future. Why categorizing needed? Because it's cool, it will sound same as a type of character in psychology, like "I'm a melancholic". Or same as diet preference, like "I'm vegan". That category you will keep in mind, and it doesn't matter what category you belong to, as long as you keep it in mind - you are being aware of what is going on around your digital space.

First Category: "Game"

"Game" traditional meaning I am referring to is - wild mammals or birds hunted for sport or food.

So "Game" people are regular users of devices. It's just, they are usually unaware of what is going on. Their common usage of digital devices is not limited, and that makes them willing to use every cool gadget and buy extra cloud storage for their photos, because they are a bit lazy or just tired of deleting pics to empty the space on hard drive. They make pics of everything they do and post them on social networks right away to get as many likes as possible,which actually eliminates time for analysis whether it is safe or not to share such picture or blogpost (maybe there is a boarding pass present in the pic, or passport, or something with other sensitive information). They use every new cool payment system and open whatever account possible to trade their favorite cryptocurrency, even if the crypto exchange was founded yesterday in a country that they won't even be able to show on map. They leave laptops opened, home wifi router without password, and if there's a password, it is usually 1234ish.

Second Category: "Turnskin"

"Turnskin" meaning someone who can change their skin at will, like in those "Werewolf" movies.

Turnskins are aware of what is going on. They have a strategy for their device usage. They allow all the digital services to watch and listen to them. They keep their passwords strong and keep a copy of all passwords in the cloud or in the email under "no subject". It is usually hard to retrieve those passwords for them as they keep forgetting where it was saved. When they want some privacy - they turn off most of the electronics and do their stuff. They are afraid that their friends and colleagues will call them "paranoid" if they offer to turn off devices if the subject of the dialogue is very sensitive. They surf the web with VPN and clear browsing history every session. They talk to others to raise awareness in digital security, but not too much, mostly as a small talk during lunch break. They are willing to keep everything secure but don't have time for enough research, and don't have enough discipline to keep everything in order.

Third Category: "Warrior"

Warrior is not perfect. Warrior lives in "continuous improvement" state. Warrior knows it is never 100% safe, warrior makes sure it is 99% safe. Warrior knows, that asking people to turn off devices for private talk is a long conversation, thats why Warrior has a cell signal blocking device handy (that's a spy one). Warriors aware if it is legal or illegal to protect themselves in digital world, and therefore act accordingly. Warriors have no interest in explaining others what to do with their digital security principles. Because Warriors keep in mind that Digital Security is every person's own responsibility. Warrior is constantly researching for modern non-linear ways to protect their privacy. Warriors block signal instead of turning off signal, when possible. Warriors are sharing their knowledge with curious people when people need advice on what to do to stay 99% safe. Warriors know, that jokes about their "paranoid" activity are actually funny, but jokes shouldn't be the reason of canceling their digital self-protection activity. Warriors have strategy. Warriors use stratagems and tactics to avoid data spills.

PART 10. MY DIGITAL SE-CURITY PRINCIPLES.

So what are the Digital Security Principles in my opinion? It is a set of principles that helps to create a tactic to move towards Warrior category.

a) Block the signal instead of turning it off.

b) Limit permissions for your apps.

c) Minimize data production.

d) Keep passwords strong.

e) Use cash.

f) Examine premises.

g) Destroy sensitive information.

h) Get a private cryptocurrency wallet from trusted source.

i) Use VPN for Internet browsing.

j) Get familiar with Dark web.

k) Never trust an email from unknown source.

l) Use separate device for sensitive information exchange.

m) Get an antivirus software.

n) Set up firewall on all of your devices' operating systems.

o) Protect your data online.

p) Keep sensitive digital data disconnected from internet.

q) Reset Advertising ID or disable if possible.

r) Stay offline as much time as possible.

s) If someone requesting data - double check the requestor's origin.

t) Encrypt everything.

u) Delete digital services apps if not using.

v) Use prepaid debit cards, buy them for cash.

w) Mask your identity while checking out new digital service.

x) Use old-school methods to keep sensitive data.

y) Remember that any word coming out of your mouth, and any tap of your finger and any click of your mouse is DATA produced.

z) Remember that your cybersecurity is your own responsibility.

Now lets repeat with more details.

a) Block the signal instead of turning off.

Cameras need light to capture something, block the light, cover every camera you have on every device. It is sometimes hard, as device makers made sure you can't do this easily or it will make your device looking odd. Thank god, there are many device cases or stickers that are made specifically to cover cameras. Just look it up on Internet.

Microphones are not easily blockable with case or a sticker. But almost every device has following logic: If you connect external microphone to your device - your device gives privilege to that external microphone over it's native internal microphone. There are so called "Mic-blocks" - small gadgets you can get online and connect to your laptop or phone to make your device think you connected external microphone, that device is only impersonating as microphone but actually not acting as one.

GPS settings you can only turn off on the device. You probably can not use "GPS signal jammers" that are there for sale. These are illegal to use in many countries, please do your homework for that. Your device's fingerprint sensor is basically a scanner that won't be able to see your fingerprint through a non-clear sticker.

Another conciderable example of signal blocker for most mobile devices is a so called Faraday case or Faraday bag. Faraday bags are based on Faraday cage technology that is cage made of flexible metallic fabric. These bags are used in criminal investigations in data storage facilities to prevent from data remote wiping on stored devices, gathered during investigation. You can also use it to protect your device from wireless data theft.

Many home based devices are using wifi when you nnnnn-nnnnare at home and also when you are not at home. Devices such as TV, any home AI, smart lights ad so on. How do you block them when you don't want them to record? I found an option - it is a simple surge protector, it's just using Wi-Fi so you can turn it on or off, using your smartphone. So when you connect your device to that surge protector - you can turn off that device by turning off surge protector, this way your device won't get any power. No power - no recording, unless it's battery operated.

b) Limit permissions for your apps.

Every app you install on any of your devices has a list of permissions that it either has them set by default or you can set permissions manually. On devices, types of permissions are separated in your device settings and in your app settings. So check both (app's and general) settings for permissions. Provide only permissions needed for functionality you are looking to use. If you no longer need to use such functionality - disable every permission associated to that functionality.

c) Minimize data production

When signing up for new service there are many required and many optional fields. Don't fill optional if there's no real need. Examine required fields, they may look like something you don't think you want to share, or something you think filling does not make sense. I usually try to put a misprinted information of that is something not important for my experience and I know it is being used for simply data harvesting purposes.

d) Keep passwords strong

Strong password is a must. Don't be angry when services ask for specific strong password. Just make sure it has everything: lowercase letter, upper case letter, number and a special character. Just use your own logic (or no logic) when creating password for any service, I use something associated with the service when I want to keep main phrase the same. For example I use 1234_Rock$_$ervice1, and for another one I use 1234_Rock$_$ervice2

e) I use cash.

I use cash for gas - it's cheaper this way. I use cash for groceries. I use cash wherever cash is accepted. I do not use cash for donations.

f) Examine premises.

When you travel you never know what laws the country you visit have. Maybe it's ok to record your private space. There are plenty of gadgets that can locate any hidden recording devices in the room. Do your own research on that topic. Also check the laws if it's permitted to use such devices.

g) Destroy sensitive information

That bill in mail you get from your water company, or credit card promotion mail from the bank. Anything made of paper. There is paper shredder invented for that.

If you store any sensitive data that you only kept because you needed to send it a year ago for authentication purposes -

erase it already. If you need it you can always create it for any purpose again. No need to keep a copy of your Drivers license for nothing, in either digital or physical form.

h) Get a private cryptocurrency wallet from trusted source.

Just get one, so when time comes you will not need to spend time creating it. Make sure it comes from trusted source. Usually those organizations that create or promote cryptocurrency - provide a wallet for it. It is better to not to keep your wallet on your device. Keep it on flash drive so it stays offline and when you need it online - you can connect it to your device.

i) Use VPN for browsing.

VPN stands for Virtual Private Network.

There are paid and free services available online, some internet browsers have free built-in VPN service.

How does VPN work? Whenever you browsing on the net, first - your device connects to your internet service provider (ISP). ISP redirects you to the website you want to visit. At that time any traffic data you create goes thought your ISP's servers. This way ISP's can see and log all your online activity. It is physically possible for ISP to hand that data to all kinds of third parties, including advertisers and government agencies. Hackers could also hack your ISP and get that data.

When you use VPN - it basically redirects all your traffic to a remote server, configured specifically for that purpose. That makes your IP address masked and also your traffic data encrypted. Encrypted means when someone try to intercept and read that data - they will see a bunch of nonsense symbols, that are not readable.

j) Get familiar with Dark web.

Just read some information on what it is and how to properly access it - it is not necessary useful, but good to know since it exists, like you know there are black holes in the universe and there are observatories where people can actually see them.

k) Never trust an email from unknown source.

Phishing is very popular amongst hackers. The email could look like your credit card banking regular email with the link to log in. Do not click links. I know it's easier, but it is always good to just go through a regular "sign-in" routine.

l) Use separate device for sensitive information exchange.

Prepaid phones are popular for people who do not want their conversations to be associated with them. This way even recorded information like text or speech has less value since it is not connected to a particular person. Advertisers won't be able to create a new file associated to you. Just don't keep your main device around while you using your secondary one.

m) Get an antivirus software.

Antiviruses help detect viruses on your computer. And sometimes even prevent viruses to be installed. Do your research for good antivirus. You can also control permissions for antiviruses - keep that in mind. If you are using your device offline for strictly storage purposes and all files transferred there are legit - no need to install antivirus. At least I do not see the reason.

n) Set up firewall.

Firewall helps to keep traffic usage limited for installed apps. Like if it wants to send out information somewhere away from your device - you will be notified and asked if you're allowing that data transfer.

o) Protect your data online.

Your cloud accounts, email and other resources are now offering 2FA. 2FA means two-factor authentication. They do this for purpose. Because they keep on fighting hackers who access accounts of their users. 2FA sends code to your phone or email when you or someone else is trying to access your account. This way that someone won't be able to log in with just knowing your username and password. Turn on 2FA where available.

Your credit report file's best state is a locked state. Only unlock it when you are applying for something.

p) Keep sensitive digital data disconnected from internet.

If you have a separate external hard drive or flash drive, then I would recommend using it for storing any sensitive data, not on your device. Device can be lost, stolen, hacked, traced. External hard drives and flash can't. Unless they have wireless connectivity device installed. I would get one without any Wi-Fi or Bluetooth option. I like wires.

q) Reset Advertising ID or disable if possible.

Most modern devices have advertising ID's. A temporary

files that provide your online activity data to 3rd parties. So third parties can properly advertise to you. You can't disable it. As far as I know - you can only reset it. I wish someone creates an app for disabling that option. There are plenty of manuals online on how to reset it. It is better to do it frequently.

r) Stay offline.

Some apps could work offline. Like your email. You can update it and then turn off Wi-Fi, and read the contents of the email. You can use free online GPS app, but you can download a paid offline one.

s) If someone is requesting your data - double check the requestors origin.

Have you received that scam call, telling something about your tax return troubles and asking for SSN? If they really seem legit you can always visit official webpage and check for the correct phone number to call back. Also, usually it is the businesses policy - not to allow their employees to ask for such sensitive information over the phone.

t) Encrypt everything.

Encrypting means just using logic to decode real purpose of your data. When you save a Drivers license picture on your device, name it something different, unrelated, like for example "logo", so hackers won't notice it is something valuable in case of data breach.

u) Delete digital services if not using.

I know it is too uncomfortable, but you can delete app every time you don't use it. And install every time you use it. Why not?

v) Use prepaid debit cards, buy them for cash.

Prepaid card could be purchased anonymously for cash in some countries. Prepaid cards have certain amount of cash pre-loaded there, so it eliminates chances of someone stealing all your money from actual checking account. It also helps to pay for services where you are not sure, if services are legit. I know many cases when someone requested an acne solution to try for $30 and got a charge of $150 after 5 months for additional kit, with no explanation, no email, nothing. And it was hard to get that money back.

w) Mask your identity to checkout new digital service.

When signing up for new service, you can go through many steps: step one - name and address, step two card information, step three - your private data. So you decided to not to go further and not share the private data. Guess what, you already shared your name and card, and there's no way to cancel that. If you see many steps and not sure whether service is legit or will ask for extra information that you don't want to share - just create a mockup profile with fake data to pass through all the steps to see what are those steps first, then share your data if you feel comfortable.

x) Use old-school methods to keep sensitive data

Notebook. It's made of paper. It stays in your house. What are the chances of hackers rob your house. Very low. What are chances hackers rob your online service - low, but not very low.

You could keep all usernames online, and keep all passwords in your notebook. In case you are forgetting your hard to guess password. Some people would say it is not safe. Up to you.

y) Remember, my friend, that any word coming out of your mouth, and any screen tap of your finger and any click of your mouse is DATA produced.

z) Remember, that your cybersecurity is your own responsibility.

Oh, by the way, I mentioned somewhere in the book I will write about "what else data equals to". Data equals to vulnerability, the more data you produce - the more vulnerable you become, emotionally, physically and digitally.

www.ingramcontent.com/pod-product-compliance
Lightning Source LLC
Chambersburg PA
CBHW031230050326
40689CB00009B/1536